Test Pattern

Basket of Flowers

PLATE 1

PLATE 1

tulip

PLATE 2

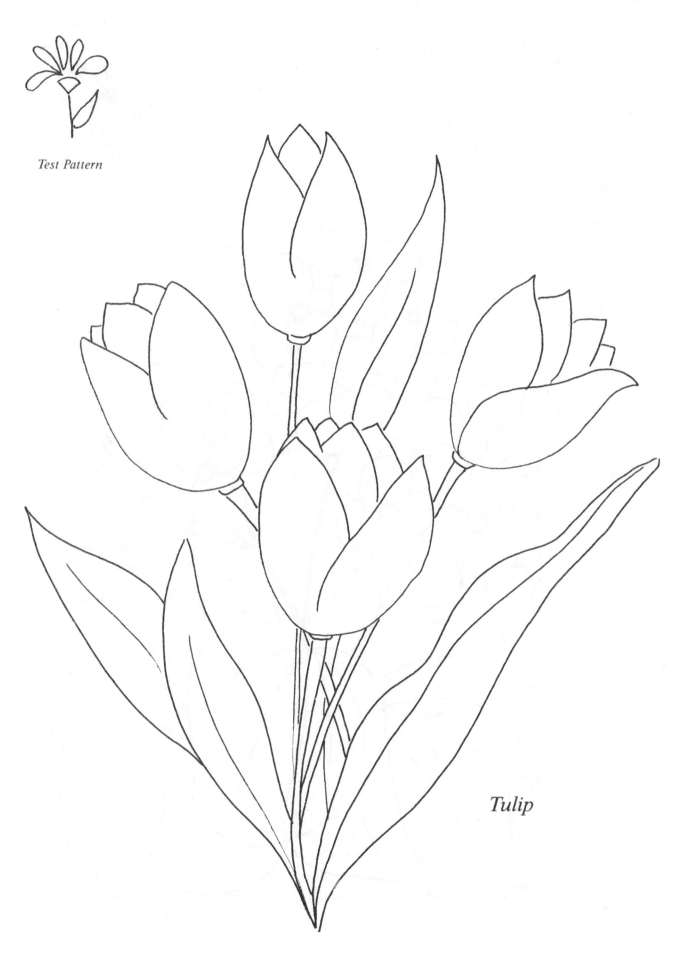

Test Pattern

Tulip

PLATE 2

Test Pattern

Geranium

PLATE 3

Geranium

PLATE 6

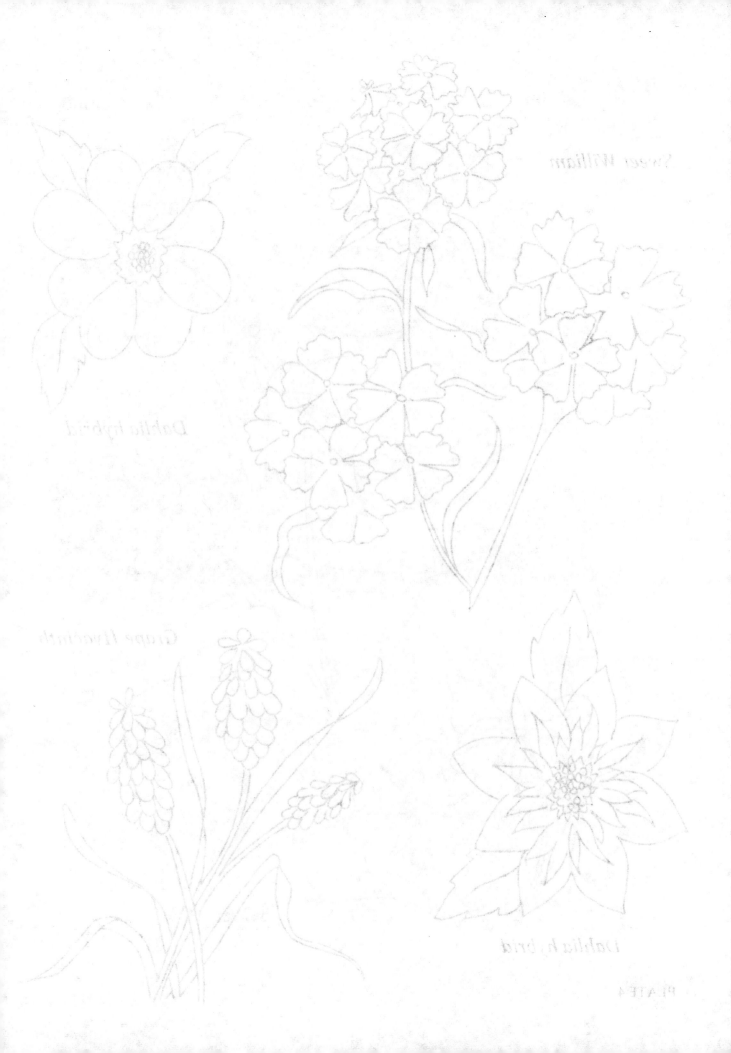

Sweet William

Dahlia hybrid

Grape Hyacinth

Dahlia hybrid

PLATE 4

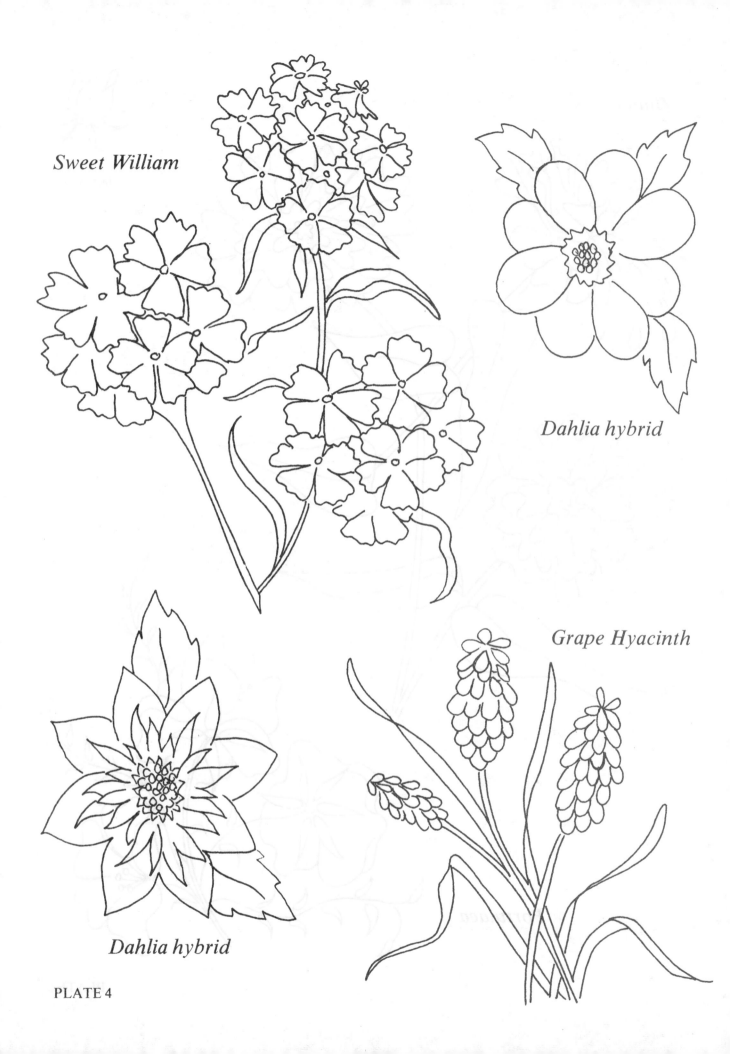

Sweet William

Dahlia hybrid

Dahlia hybrid

Grape Hyacinth

PLATE 4

Zinnia

Test Pattern

Portulaca

PLATE 5

1st Pattern

Portulaca

PLATE 5

Test Pattern

Gladiolus

Hollyhock

PLATE 6

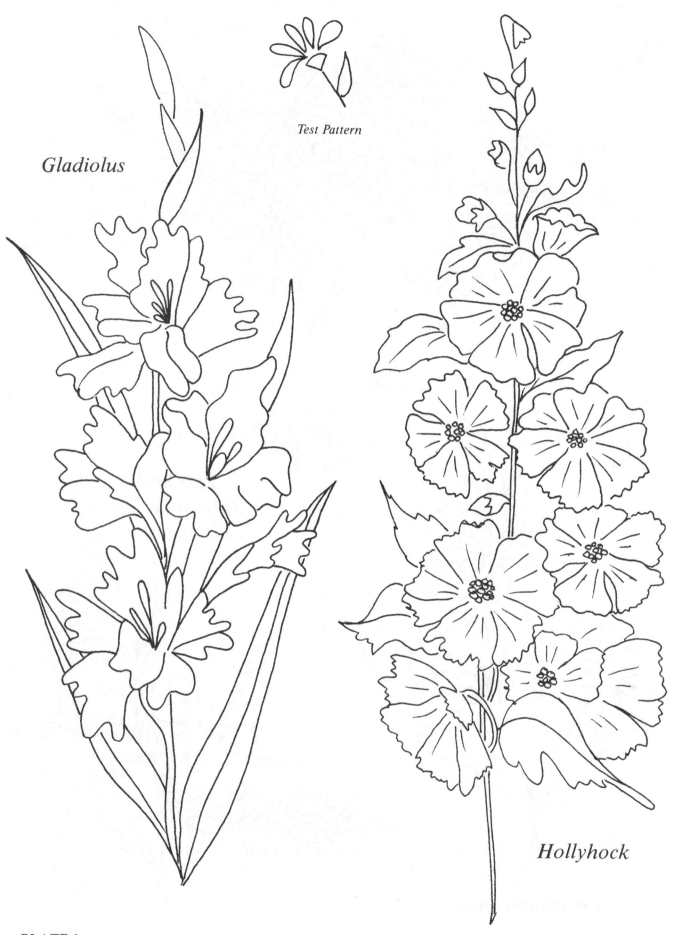

Gladiolus

Test Pattern

Hollyhock

PLATE 6

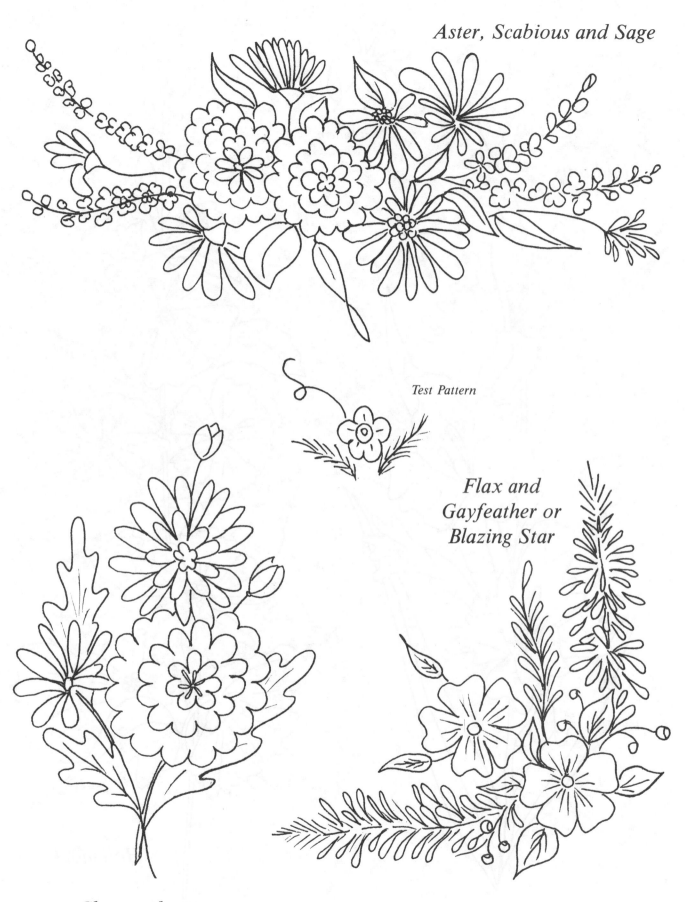

Aster, Scabious and Sage

Test Pattern

*Flax and
Gayfeather or
Blazing Star*

Chrysanthemum

PLATE 7

Tea Tarm

Flax and
Gayfeather or
Blazing Star

Chrysanthemum

PLATE 7

Rose

PLATE 5

Test Pattern

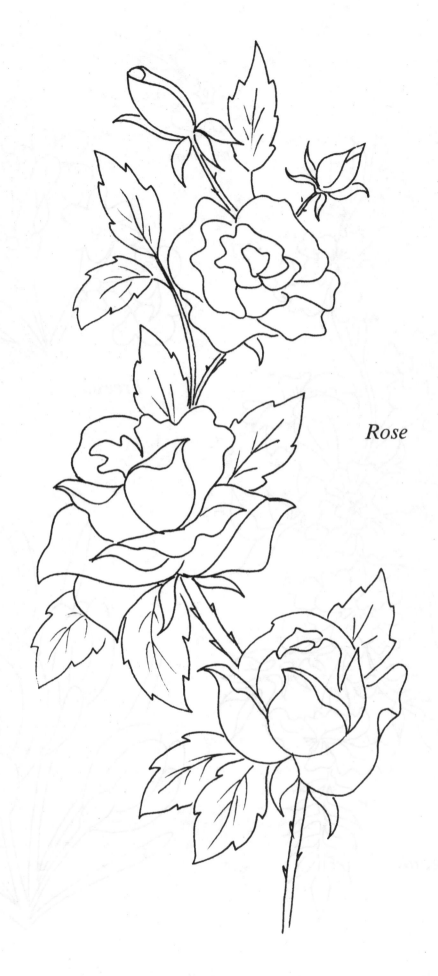

Rose

PLATE 8

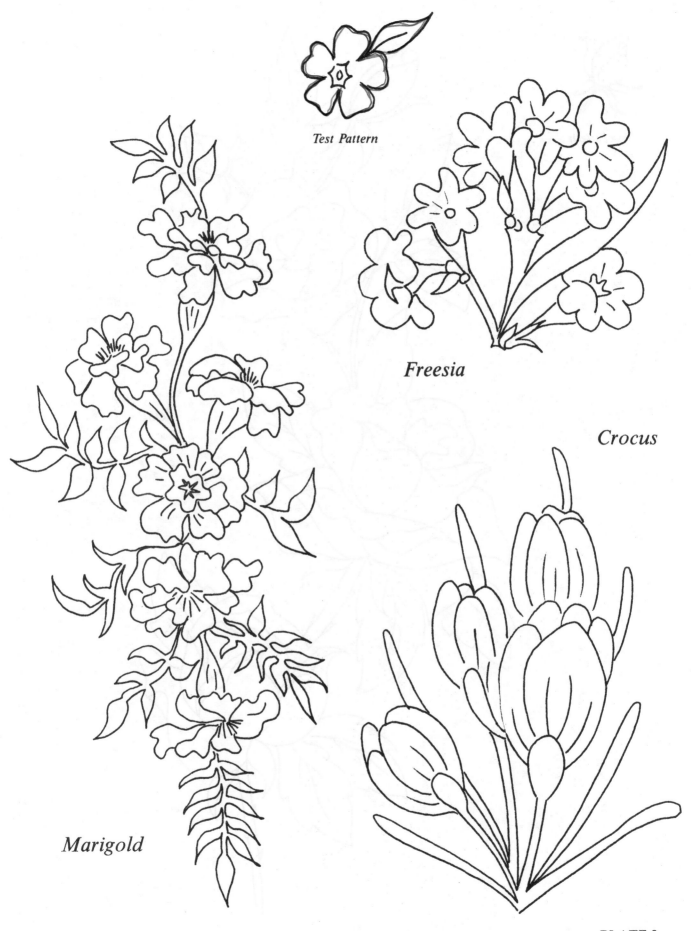

Test Pattern

Freesia

Crocus

Marigold

PLATE 9

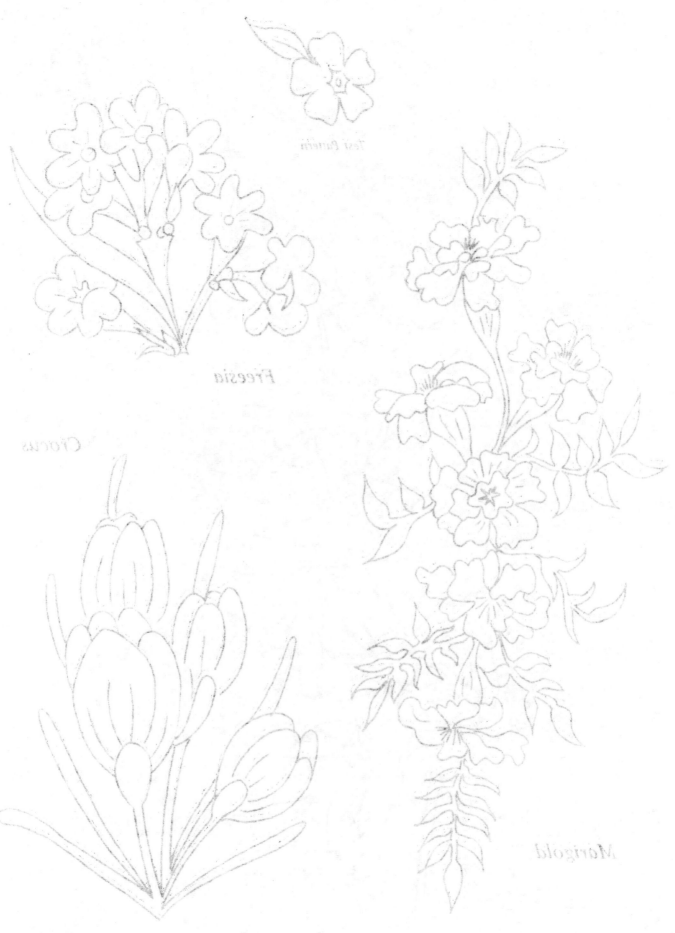

Test Pattern

Freesia

Crocus

Marigold

PLATE 9

PLATE 10

Test Pattern

Garden Flower Bouquet

PLATE 10

Daffodil

Test Pattern

PLATE 11

Daffodil

Tea Plant

PLATE II

Sweet Pea,
Daffodil,
Carnation and
Snapdragon

Tea Pansy.

Lily-of-the-Valley,
Forget-me-not,
Sweet Alyssum and
Rockfoil.

PLATE 12

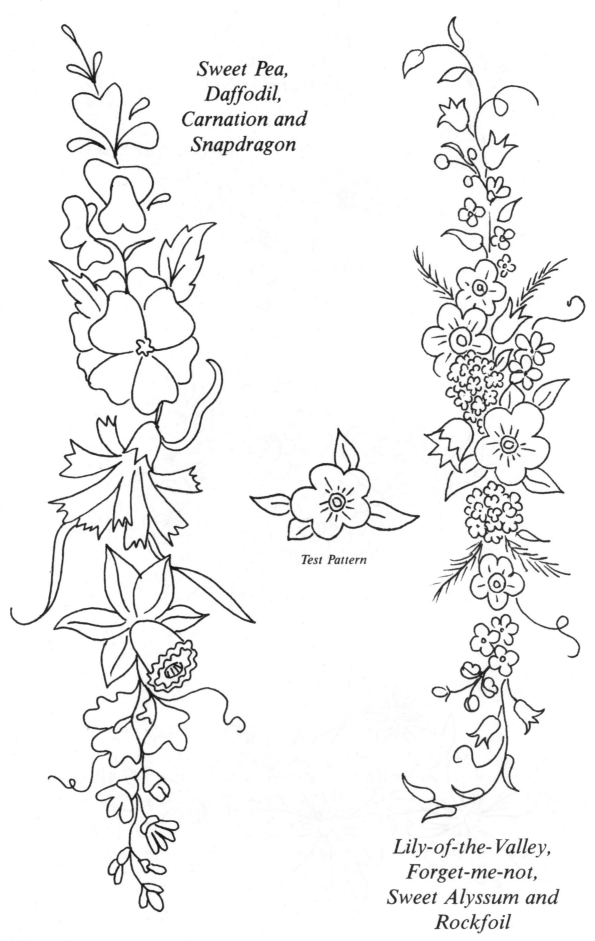

*Sweet Pea,
Daffodil,
Carnation and
Snapdragon*

Test Pattern

*Lily-of-the-Valley,
Forget-me-not,
Sweet Alyssum and
Rockfoil*

PLATE 12

Daisy, Pink and Wormwood

Marigold

Bitter-root

PLATE 13

Marigold

Bitter-root

Daisy, Pink, and Wormwood

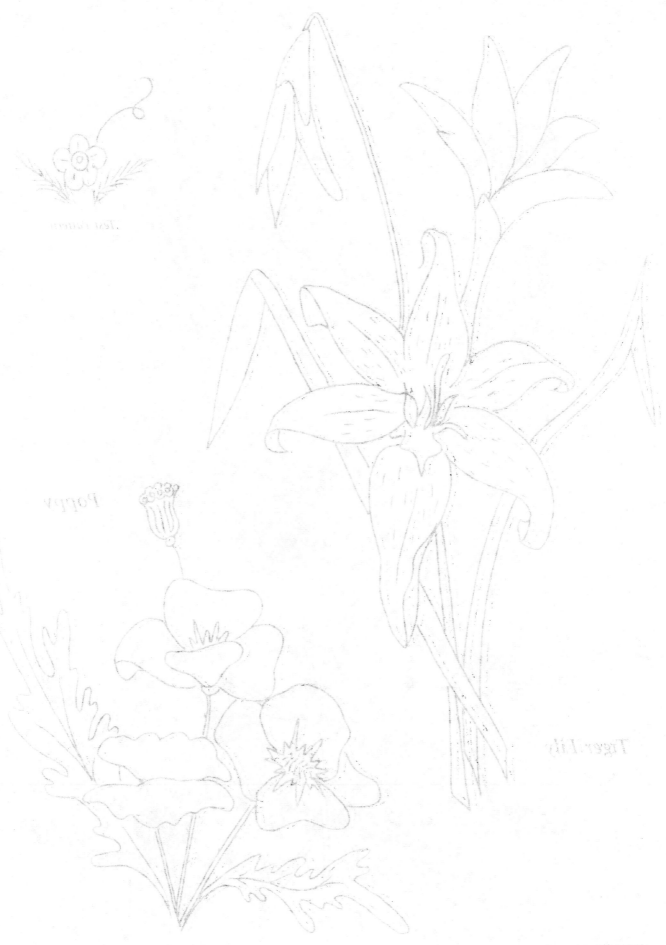

Tea-flower

Poppy

Tiger-Lily

PLATE 24

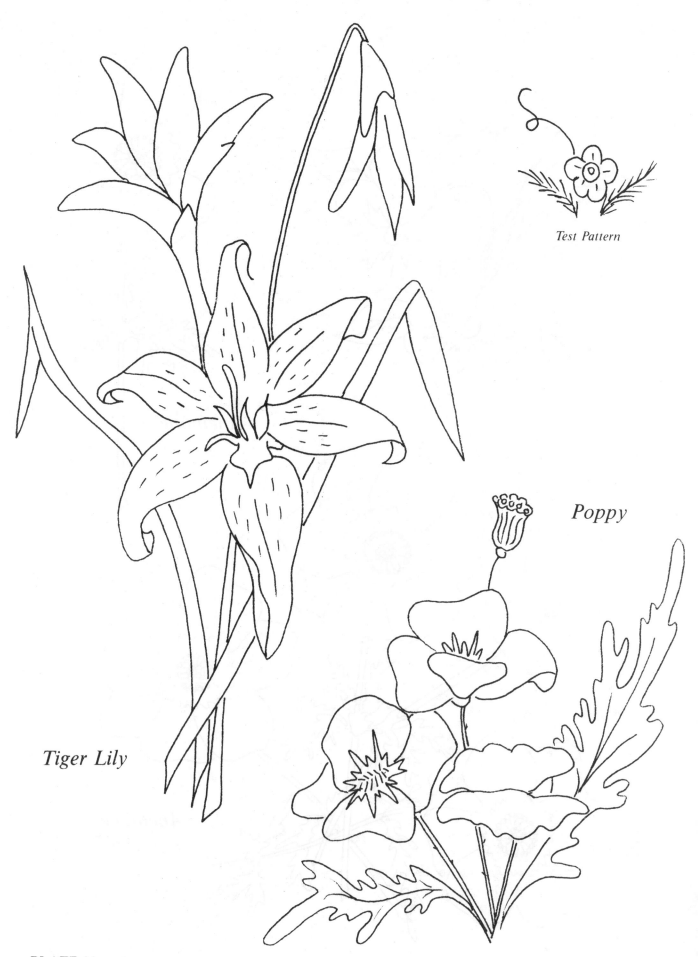

Test Pattern

Poppy

Tiger Lily

PLATE 14

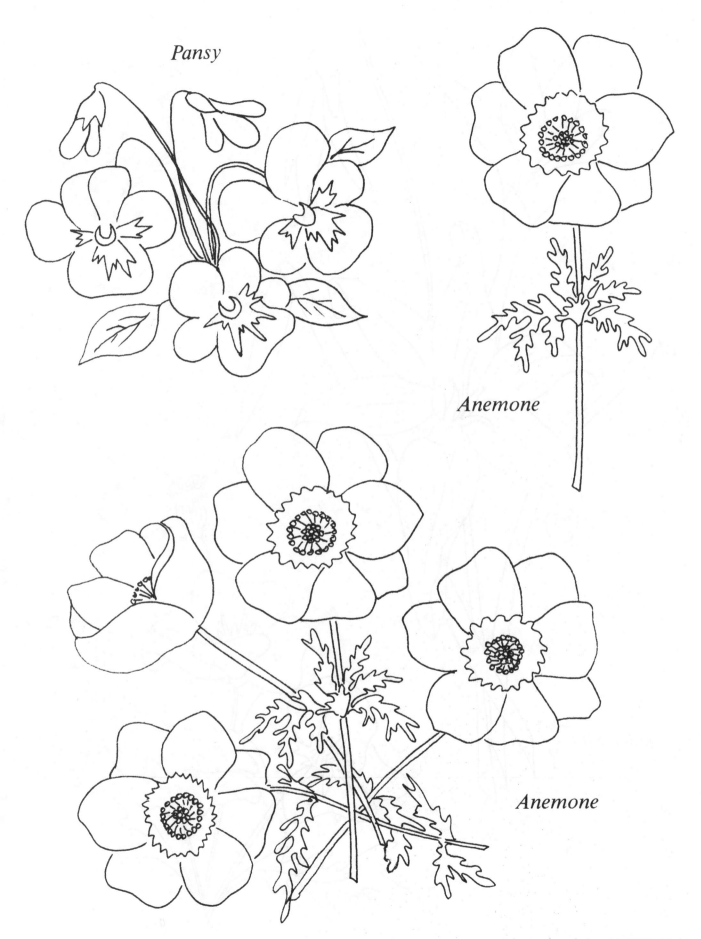

Pansy

Anemone

Anemone

PLATE 15

Pansy

Anemone

Anemone

PLATE 15

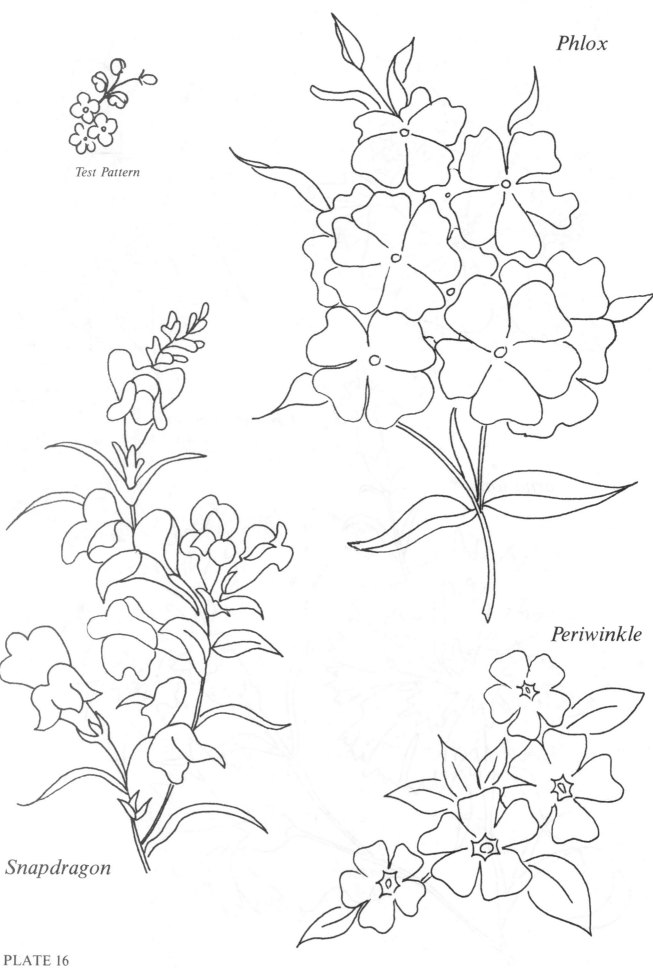

Phlox

Test Pattern

Periwinkle

Snapdragon

PLATE 16

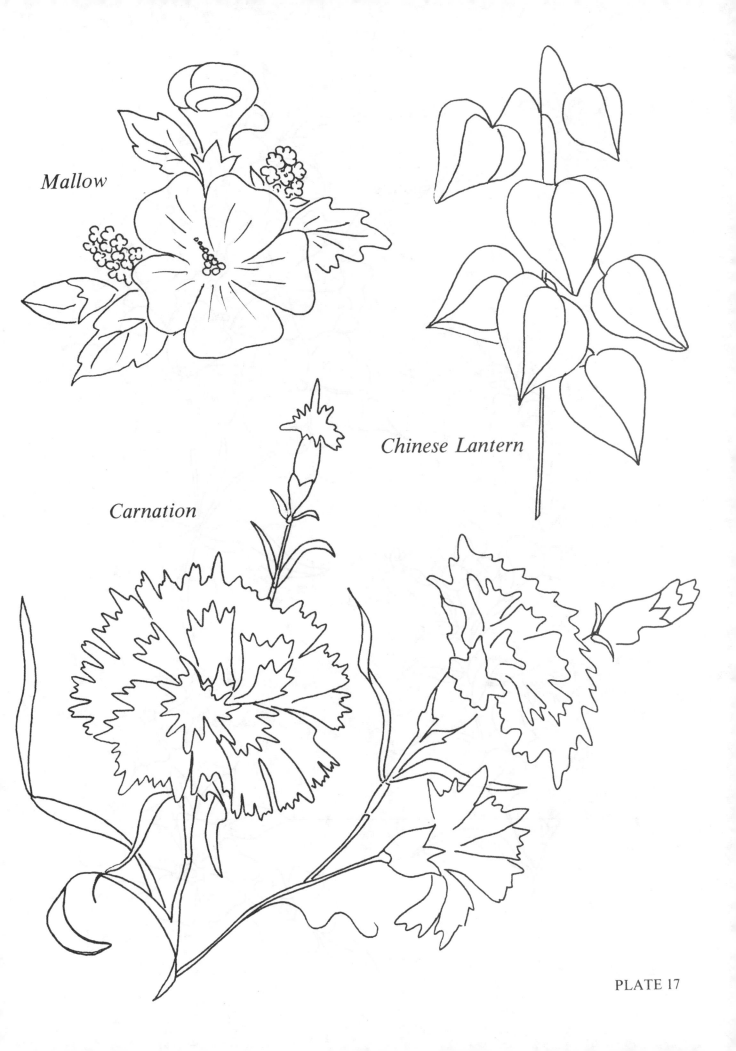

Mallow

Chinese Lantern

Carnation

PLATE 17

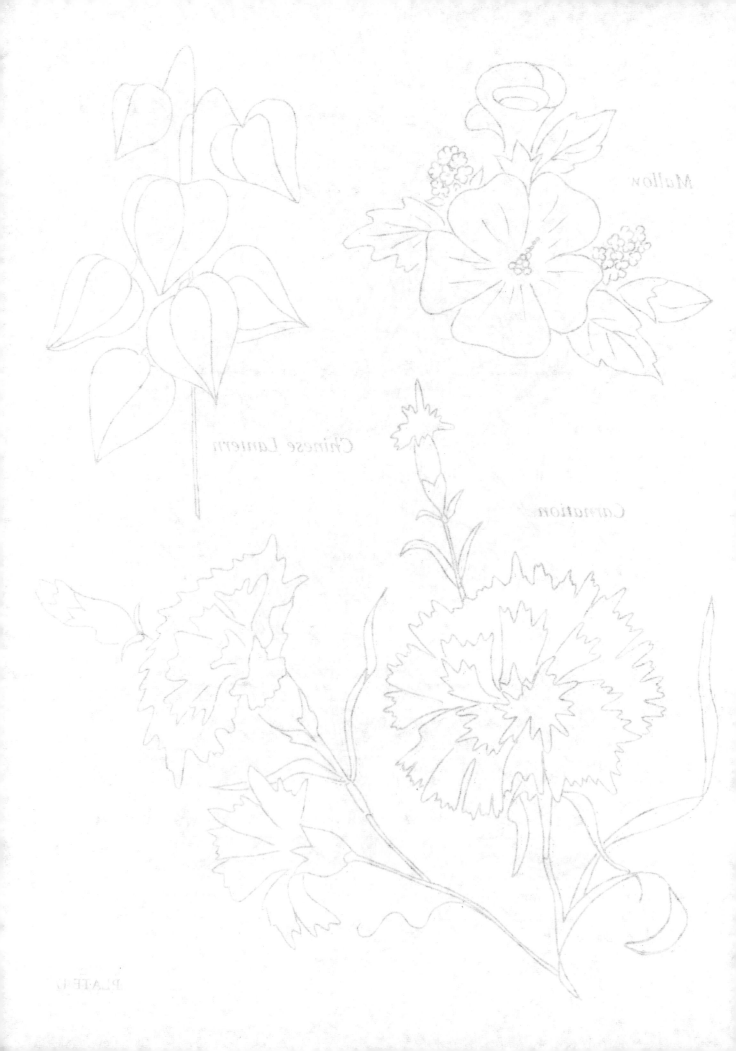

Mallow

Chinese Lantern

Carnation

PLATE I.

Nasturtium

Test Pattern

Nasturtium

PLATE 18

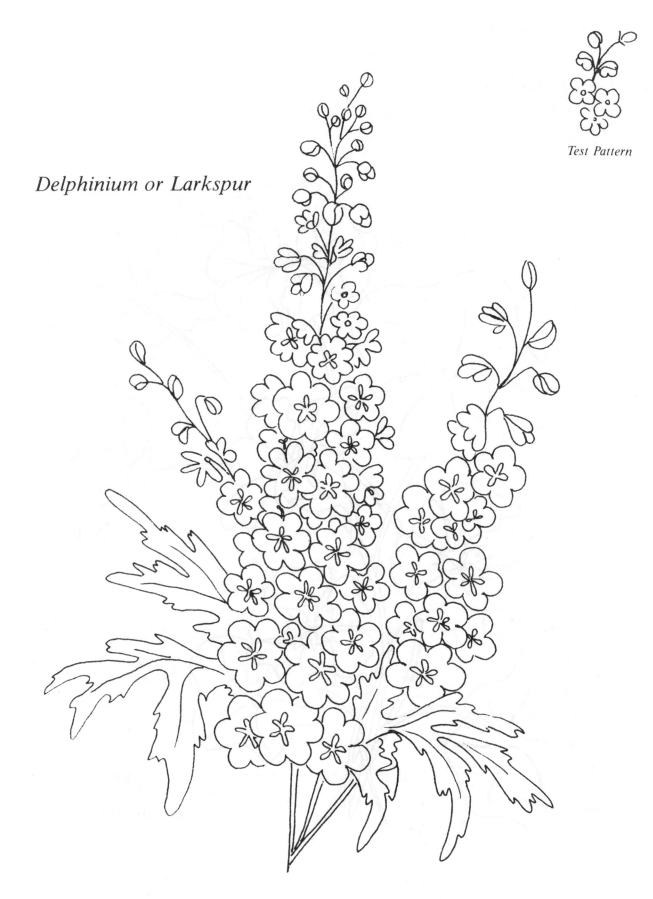

Delphinium or Larkspur

PLATE 19

Delphinium or Larkspur

Tree Larkspur

PLATE 39

PLATE 39

Gaillardia

Hyacinth

Spring Snowflake

PLATE 20

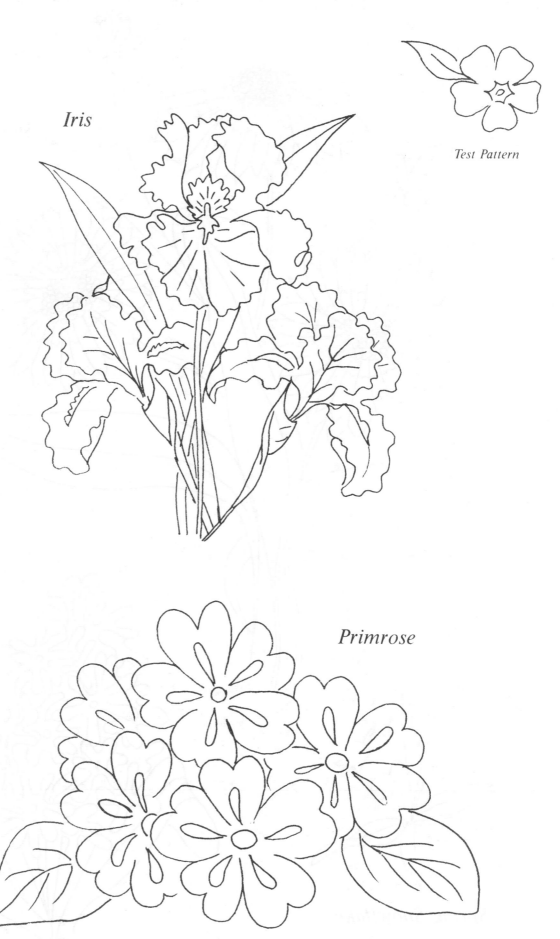

Iris

Test Pattern

Primrose

PLATE 21

PLATE 21

Chrysanthemum.

Cornflower.

Pæ.. nes

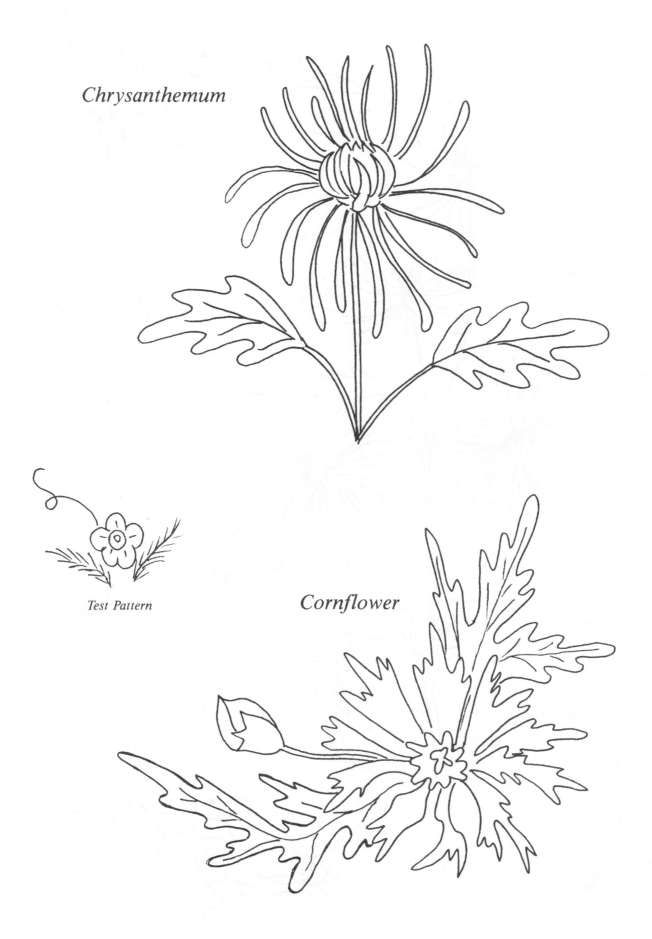

Chrysanthemum

Test Pattern

Cornflower

PLATE 22

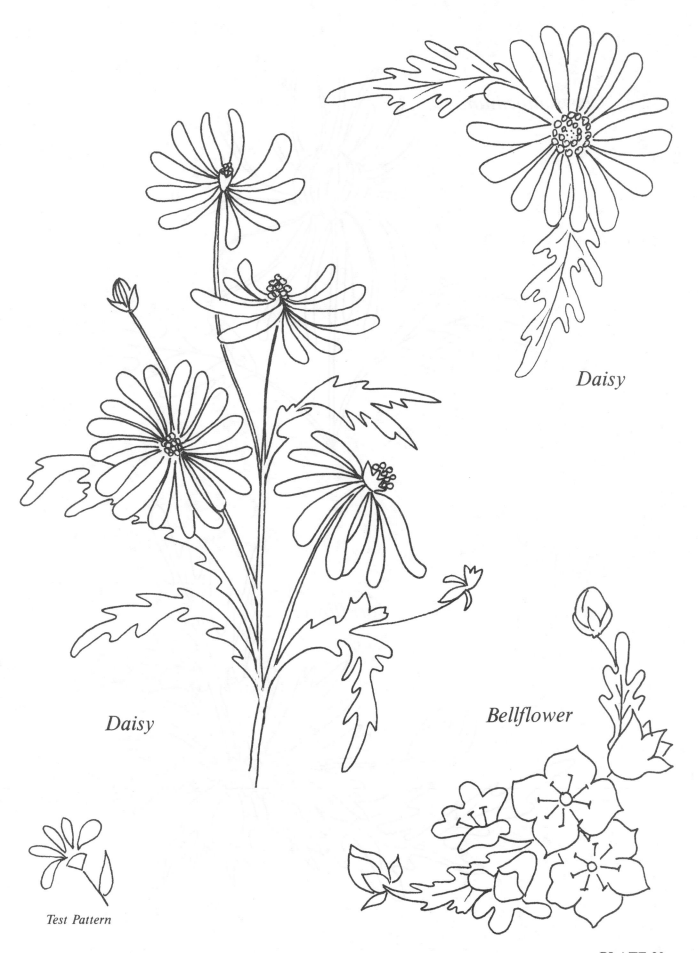

Daisy

Daisy

Test Pattern

Bellflower

PLATE 23

Daisy

Bellflower

Daisy

Test Pattern

PLATE 23

Day Lily

PLATE 24